SHOCKWAVE

SOCIAL STUDIES

MYSTERIOUS PLACES

Sue Adasiewicz

SCHOLASTIC

This 2009 British adaptation published by
Scholastic Ltd
Villiers House
Clarendon Avenue
Leamington Spa
Warwickshire CV32 5PR

British Library Cataloguing-in-Publication Data.
A catalogue record for this book is available from the British Library.
ISBN 978-1407-10130-9

Author: Sue Adasiewicz
Educational Consultants: Ian Morrison and Nikki Gamble
Editors: Nerida Frost, Marion Archer and Simret Brar
Designer: Steve Clarke
Photo Researcher: Jamshed Mistry

Photographs by: Aapimage.com: AP (p. 1); **Blake Wells** (pp. 10–11); **Getty Images** (p. 29; Stonehenge, pp. 30–31); **Jennifer and Brian Lupton** (teenagers, pp. 30–31); **www. BrownMountainLights.com** (Brown Mountain Lights, p. 21); **Photolibrary** (cover; pp. 6–7; upright Easter Island statue, p. 15; pp. 22–23; pp. 26–27); **Russ Bodnar/United States National Park Service** (Fajada Butte, p. 9); © **Solstice Project, photograph by Alan Price** (rock slabs, pp. 8–9); **Stockxpert** (Stonehenge diagram, p. 23); **Tranz: Corbis** (p. 5; pp. 12–13; Easter Island quarry, p. 15; pp. 16–17; lightning, *Pride of Baltimore II*, pp. 18–19; Blue Ridge Mountains, pp. 20–21; aerial view of Kukulcan, p. 25); **Reuters** (waterspout, pp. 18–19)

The publisher would like to thank Blake Wells for the photograph of Ringing Rocks on pages 10–11.

1 2 3 4 5 6 7 8 9   9 0 1 2 3 4 5 6 7 8

Printed in China through Colorcraft Ltd., Hong Kong

CONTENTS

HIGH-POWERED WORDS

assume to accept that something is true without checking it

astronomy the study of stars, planets and space

ceremony an event held to mark a special occasion

geoglyph a drawing made on the ground

logic thinking that involves reasoning and following steps to reach correct answers

petroglyph a carving or drawing made on rock

phenomena events or facts that can be seen, felt or experienced

For easy reference, see Wordmark on back flap.
For additional vocabulary, see Glossary on page 32.

The word *glyph* in *geoglyph* and *petroglyph* refers to a symbolic figure, usually carved or engraved. Other words using *glyph* are: *diaglyph, hieroglyph* and *lithoglyph.*

The White Horse of Uffington is on a hill near Uffington, England. The figure, 114 metres long, is cut into the turf. It is about 3000 years old.

Easter Island is a tiny island in the middle of the South Pacific Ocean. More than 600 ancient statues stand on its grassy meadows. For more than 200 years, visitors to the island have wondered about the statues. How did the statues get there? What were they for?

All over the world, there are places, such as Easter Island, that have puzzling structures. There are also places with unusual **phenomena**, such as unexplained lights. Places like these have always fascinated people. In this book, you can read about the science behind some of these mysteries. You can also find out about places that scientists are still seeking to explain.

Statues of Easter Island

Some of the World's Mysterious Places

The Sun Dagger

There is a steep, flat-topped hill in Chaco Canyon, New Mexico. Three slabs of stone are placed on it. Two spirals are carved into the rock wall behind them. What did these things mean to the people who lived there a thousand years ago?

Chaco Canyon was once a great **cultural** centre of the Pueblo people. The Pueblo lived in the area from about AD900 to AD1150. The climate was very dry. Growing crops would have been difficult. It would have been important to plant and harvest at the right times.

The three slabs of stone and the rock carvings on Fajada **Butte** may have helped the Pueblo to do this. **Archaeologists** think the site, known as the Sun Dagger, served as a calendar. However, the purpose of Chaco Canyon and the Sun Dagger is still not fully understood. Some historians think it is most likely that Chaco Canyon was used as a gathering place for **ceremonies**.

Before clocks and watches were invented, the sun was used to tell the time. The sundial of Jantar Mantar in Jaipur, India, is the world's largest. Use the internet and other sources to find out about this and other sundials.

Spirals are carved into the rock face behind the three slabs of stone.

How the Sun Dagger Worked

The Sun Dagger is made up of three slabs of stone and two spirals carved into the rock face behind the slabs. There is a large and a small spiral. Rays of sunlight fall through the cracks between the slabs onto the **petroglyphs**. Depending on the time of year, the position of the rays changes.

In the last years, the stone slabs have shifted slightly. However, before this happened, this is how the Sun Dagger worked. At the summer **solstice**, one ray of sun fell exactly on the centre of the large spiral. It looked like a dagger piercing the spiral. This is how the site got its name. At the winter solstice, two rays of sun framed the large spiral. At the **equinoxes**, a ray of sun fell on each spiral. One fell halfway between the centre and edge of the large spiral. The other ray fell directly on the small spiral.

Mystery Music

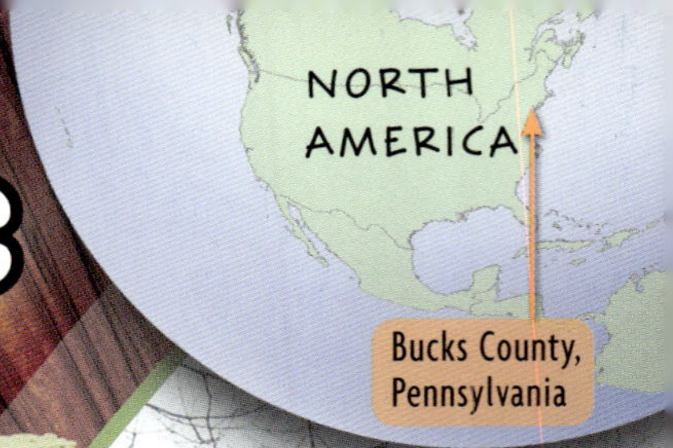

Deep in a forest in Bucks County, Pennsylvania, there is a huge clearing. It is covered with a layer of rocks three metres deep. The rocks are clear of soil and plants. When you strike some of the rocks with a hard object, they ring like bells.

Some **geologists** believe the ringing comes from pressure inside the rocks. The ringing rocks are composed of volcanic **basalt**. When water seeps into the rocks, it combines with the minerals inside the rocks to form clay. The clay takes up more space than the minerals. This causes pressure to build up.

All the rocks in the field are made up of the same iron and minerals. It is still not clear why some of the rocks ring and others do not. The rocks have different tones. They can sound like little tinkling bells, big clanging bells or gongs.

Did You Know?

In 1890, Dr JJ Ott gave one of the world's first "rock" concerts. Dr Ott collected rocks from the field in Bucks County. He found enough rocks with different tones to play several songs. He played the rocks accompanied by a brass band. Since then, many musicians have put on concerts with the ringing rocks.

Some of the rocks ring when hit with a hammer or similar object.

The heading *Mystery Music* is an example of alliteration: a repetition of the same sound at the beginning of two or more words. Other examples from the Contents page include: *Terrible Triangle, Standing Stones* and *Pyramid Puzzle.*

The Giants of Easter Island

More than 600 enormous stone statues stand on a lonely island in the South Pacific Ocean. Their huge heads stare blankly across the treeless slopes. The statues look like giants frozen in motion.

The statues of Easter Island were built between AD900 and AD1500. They were carved out of stone from one of the **extinct** volcanoes on the island. Archaeologists think that people of the island built the statues to honour their gods or their **ancestors**.

The statues are scattered all over the island. Most of them were knocked down in the late 1600s. In the last 40 years, many have been returned to their standing positions. Most of the statues are three to six metres tall. Some are 12 metres tall and weigh 90 tonnes! That is equivalent to the weight of seven double-decker buses.

AD is short for the Latin *anno Domini*. This means "in the year of our Lord" (the year Jesus is thought to have been born). Some people now use the term CE, which is short for *common era*, to describe this period.

Did You Know?

Easter Island is more than 1900 kilometres away from the nearest land. The Polynesian people of the island call it Rapanui. These people and their language are also known as Rapanui. They call the statues *moai*.

Dutch explorers came to Easter Island in 1722. Since then, people have wondered how the islanders moved the statues. We now know that Easter Island was once covered with trees. The people probably made wooden sledges and rollers to move the statues. By the late 1600s, there were no more trees left on the island, so the statues could no longer be moved.

It is not only the statues of Easter Island that fascinate archaeologists. Stone tablets with mysterious writing have also been found. No one has yet been able to decode the writing.

In 1888, Easter Island became a part of Chile. There are now more than 4000 people living there. They are working to preserve the culture of their island. They also continue to study its mysteries.

The Olmec, an ancient civilisation from Mexico, also made giant statues. Twelve carved colossal heads standing three metres tall have been discovered. Use the internet to find pictures of the heads and other artworks by the Olmec.

SHOCKER

In the late 1800s, nearly 1500 Easter Islanders were taken to Peru as slaves. Only a few came back. Many of them then died of diseases. Others left the island. By 1877, only 110 people were left on Easter Island.

Most of the statues were carved at the **quarry** at Rano Raraku. Then they were moved. Many statues still lie unfinished near the quarry today.

Some of the statues stand alone. Some stand in groups or rows. Most of the statues face inland.

Terrible Triangle

*Many people have met their **doom** in this part of the Atlantic Ocean. More than 50 ships and 20 aircraft have disappeared there in the last 100 years. Long before the area had a name, it was **shrouded** in mystery.*

It was the story of Flight 19 that gave this area off the south-eastern coast of Florida its name. On 5 December 1945, five bombers took off from a navy base in Florida. The TBM Avenger bombers and their crews were never seen again. One of the planes sent out to search for them also disappeared.

In 1964, American author Vincent Gaddis wrote about Flight 19 and other disappearances in a magazine. He came up with the name Bermuda Triangle for the area. The name turned it into a legend.

World War II TBM Avenger bombers

Did You Know?

Compasses point to magnetic north, which is not the same as true north. There can be as much as 20 degrees difference between the two. This difference must be taken into account in **navigation**. Otherwise people can get lost. However, there is a line through earth where true north and magnetic north line up. It is called the agonic line.

Magnetic north is not fixed. It slowly shifts. Therefore the agonic line also shifts. Many people think the agonic line runs through the Bermuda Triangle. They **assume** this is one reason why so many people got lost there. However, the agonic line hasn't run through the Bermuda Triangle since the late 1900s.

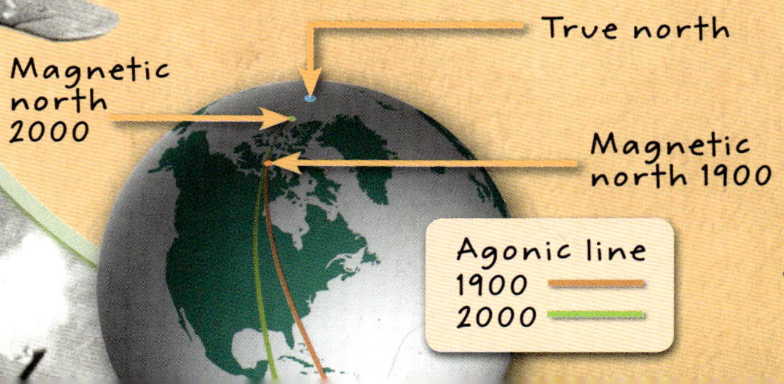

Meteorologists, the US Navy and the US Coastguard say that the Bermuda Triangle is not as mysterious as it seems. The area is known for sudden, violent storms. They can be so small that satellites don't see them. The **Gulf Stream** cuts through the Bermuda Triangle. It can create very rough seas. People often don't understand all these dangers.

It is not surprising that wreckage is rarely found in the Bermuda Triangle. It is the deepest part of the Atlantic Ocean. The Puerto Rico Trench is more than 9000 metres deep. Strong currents carry away anything that doesn't sink.

Finally, shipping and air traffic in this part of the Atlantic is very heavy. The experts say that the number of losses in the Bermuda Triangle is normal for the amount of traffic.

Ships and planes can have trouble with their radios during electrical storms.

Summarising

- read information carefully
- separate fact from opinion
- choose most suitable facts
- state your opinion
- use chosen facts to support opinion

Bermuda Triangle Survivors

In 1986, the sailing boat *Pride of Baltimore* was caught in a thunderstorm in the Bermuda Triangle. The storm was so sudden and so fierce that there was no chance to send a distress call. A huge wave knocked the boat over. Within minutes, it had sunk and four people had died.

Eight survivors waited in a life raft for four days to be rescued. During this time, two of them vowed to marry each other if they survived. John Flanagan and Leslie McNish did get married. They continued to love sailing. In fact, they brought up their two children on a sailing boat!

Waterspouts are common in the Bermuda Triangle.

Pride of Baltimore II was built after the original sailing boat sank in 1986.

The Legend of Lights

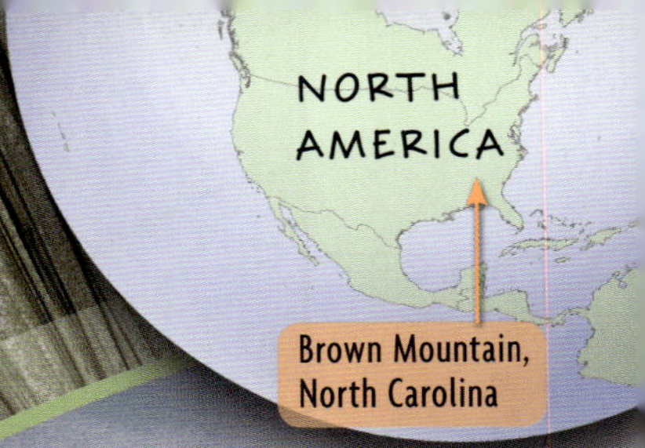

If you are near Brown Mountain, North Carolina, on a dark night, watch out for eerie lights on the mountain. They might look like bright fireballs or a soft glow. They may float slowly or whirl around. Don't be alarmed. For the past 200 years, people have talked of seeing lights on Brown Mountain.

The first accounts of the lights were in Native American legends. There are also Civil War stories about them. The first newspaper article about the lights appeared in the *Charlotte Observer* in 1913. There is no question that mysterious lights can be seen on Brown Mountain. The question is: Where do they come from?

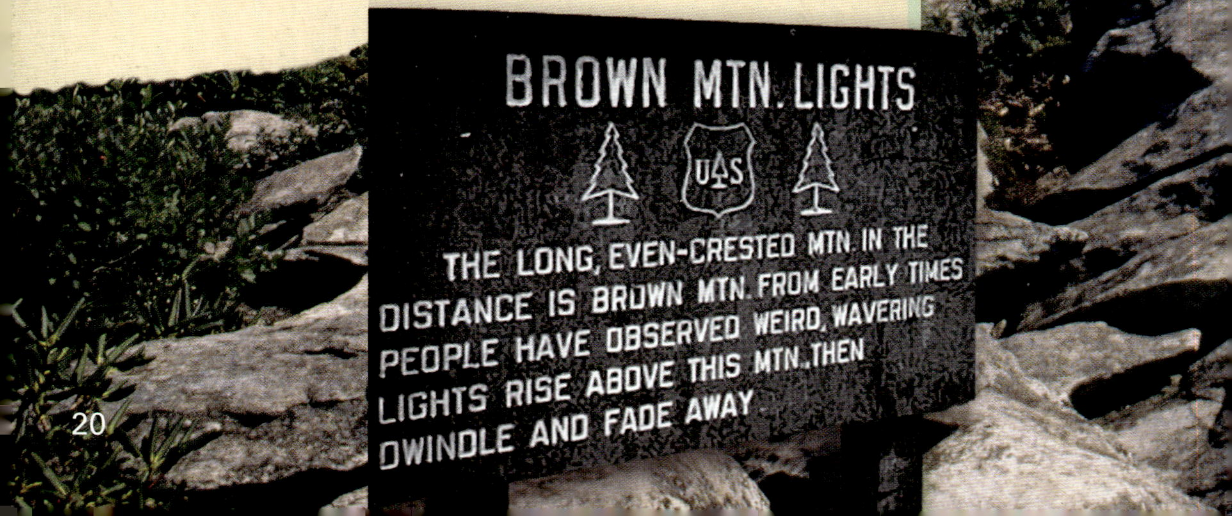

Scientific Studies

The Brown Mountain lights have been investigated by United States government organisations three times in the last 100 years. One study concluded that the lights were reflections of train or car headlights. However, the lights were seen long before the invention of cars or electric lights!

Another theory is that burning swamp gas causes the lights. However, there are no swamps in the area. Private organisations continue to study the lights. No one has found an answer for the mystery of the Brown Mountain lights.

Brown Mountain is in the Blue Ridge Mountains of North Carolina.

Brown Mountain facts

- bright fireballs or soft glow
- float or swirl
- seen for more than 200 years
- first newspaper account – 1913

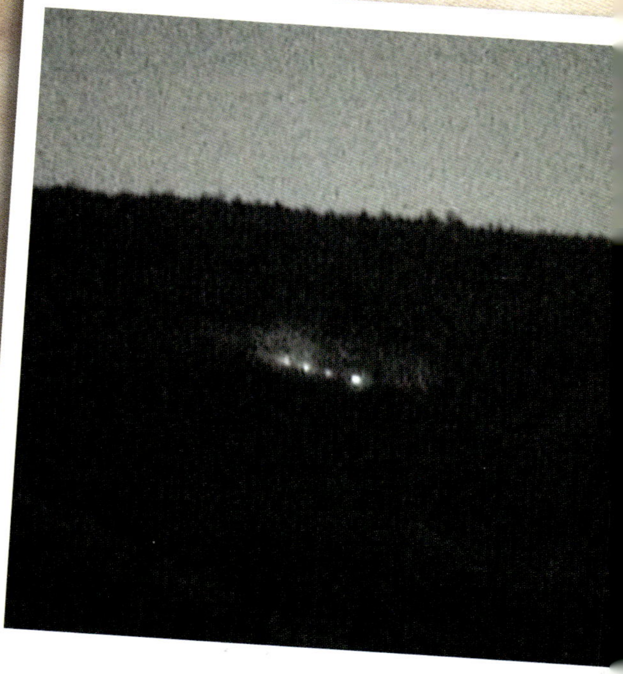

This photo of the Brown Mountain lights was taken by a private research team from Asheville, North Carolina.

Standing Stones

*A circle of giant stones stands on the Salisbury Plain in southwestern England. It is called Stonehenge. For 2500 years, people have wondered how it was built and what it was for. Prehistoric people had no wheels or animals to help them move the **monoliths**. Transporting and erecting them seems to have been nearly impossible.*

In the last 50 years, archaeologists have found out a lot about how Stonehenge was built. There was little mystery behind its construction. There was certainly an enormous amount of time and effort. The ring of large stones probably took more than 200 years to build, from about 1750BC to 1500BC. In all, Stonehenge probably took 30 million hours of work to build! Scientists believe that it would have taken about 500 people just to pull one of the giant stones a short distance.

The true mystery of Stonehenge lies in what it was built for. Some scholars think ancient people used it for **astronomy**. Others think it was a sacred site for ceremonies, burials or **sacrifices**.

Originally, Stonehenge had two full circles of stones. Inside these, there were two horseshoes of stones. The outer circle and the horseshoe of giant stones had **lintels**.

SHOCKER

In the past, many stones were taken away from Stonehenge to build bridges and dams. Tourists also chipped off pieces of the stones for souvenirs. Today, there are guards and a fence around the site to protect it.

Pyramid Puzzle

It is the spring equinox. A crowd of people stands at the foot of the ***pyramid****. Just as the sun sets, they see a fearsome sight. It looks as if a giant serpent is slithering down the steps. The sight sends a shiver through the crowd.*

The pyramid of Kukulcán stands in Chichén Itzá. It was built by the Maya around AD1000. The Maya had a great empire in Central America from about AD250 to AD1500. They were experts at mathematics and astronomy. They used this knowledge to design the pyramid to honour the serpent god, Kukulcán.

The pyramid was positioned precisely. On certain days of the year, several triangles of light and shadow could be seen on the steps. They formed a zigzag pattern. At the bottom of the steps was the carved head of a serpent. The head, along with the zigzag pattern, looked like a giant serpent.

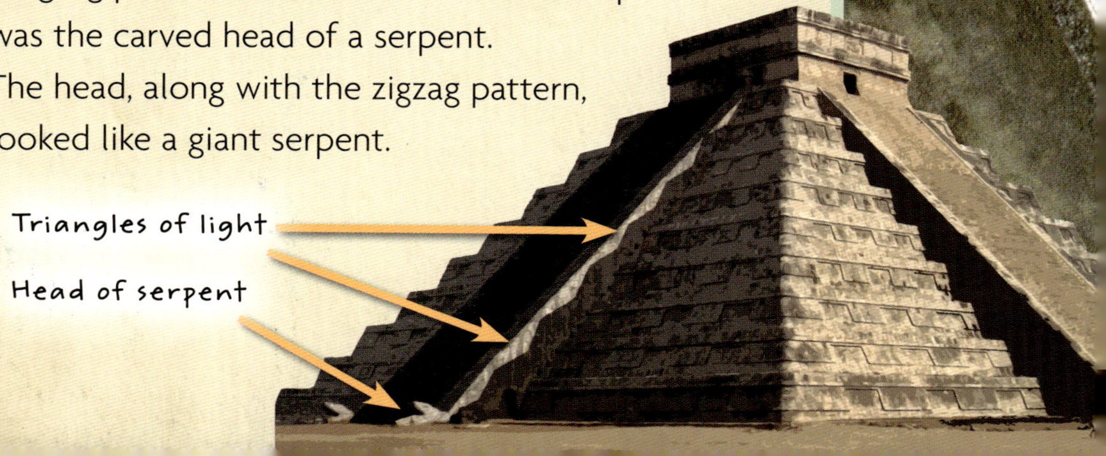

Did You Know?

Historians believe that the Maya also built the pyramid of Kukulcán to use as a calendar. It has four sides with 91 steps each. This matches the four seasons with 91 days each. The top platform could be counted as the 365th day. Each day, the shadow of the sun moved up or down one step.

SHOCKER

The Maya loved sports. One of the biggest Maya ball courts was at Chichén Itzá. Legend has it that the captain of the winning team got his head cut off. Apparently, it was a great honour to be sacrificed to the gods!

Bird's-Eye View

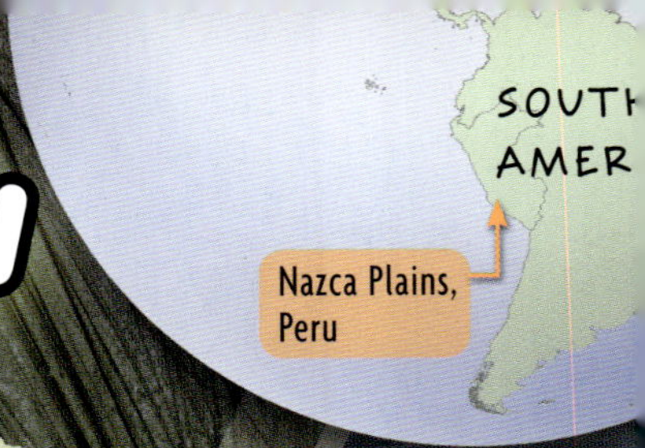

Giant lines criss-cross the Nazca Desert in southern Peru. The lines are so big that the figures they form can be seen only from the sky above them. The Nazca people made the lines between 200BC and AD600. How did the Nazca draw them without being able to see them from above? For whom did they make them?

Until the 1920s, no one recognised the **geoglyphs** as complete figures. When planes started crossing the desert, people saw the drawings of animals and geometric shapes for the first time. Scientists have shown how the lines were probably made using simple tools. However, why the Nazca made the lines is still not fully understood.

Some people believe that the Nazca lines were part of a huge star calendar. Others think they were sacred paths used for rituals. However, most scholars now think that the lines and figures were probably made for the eyes of the gods, who looked down from the heavens above.

Fact	Opinion
• geoglyphs first recognised – 1920s	• lines are a huge star calendar
• they are drawings of animals and geometric shapes	• lines were sacred paths used in rituals

The condor is a bird once common in Peru.

Did You Know?

Tourist at the Nazca lines

The lines were made by moving dark pebbles aside. This uncovered the lighter ground beneath. The desert here is dry and windless. This is why the lines have remained almost unchanged for nearly 1500 years.

The Nazca lines include more than 300 figures and lines, spread over an area of 500 square kilometres. Some of the figures are more than 120 metres long. Some of the lines are several kilometres long.

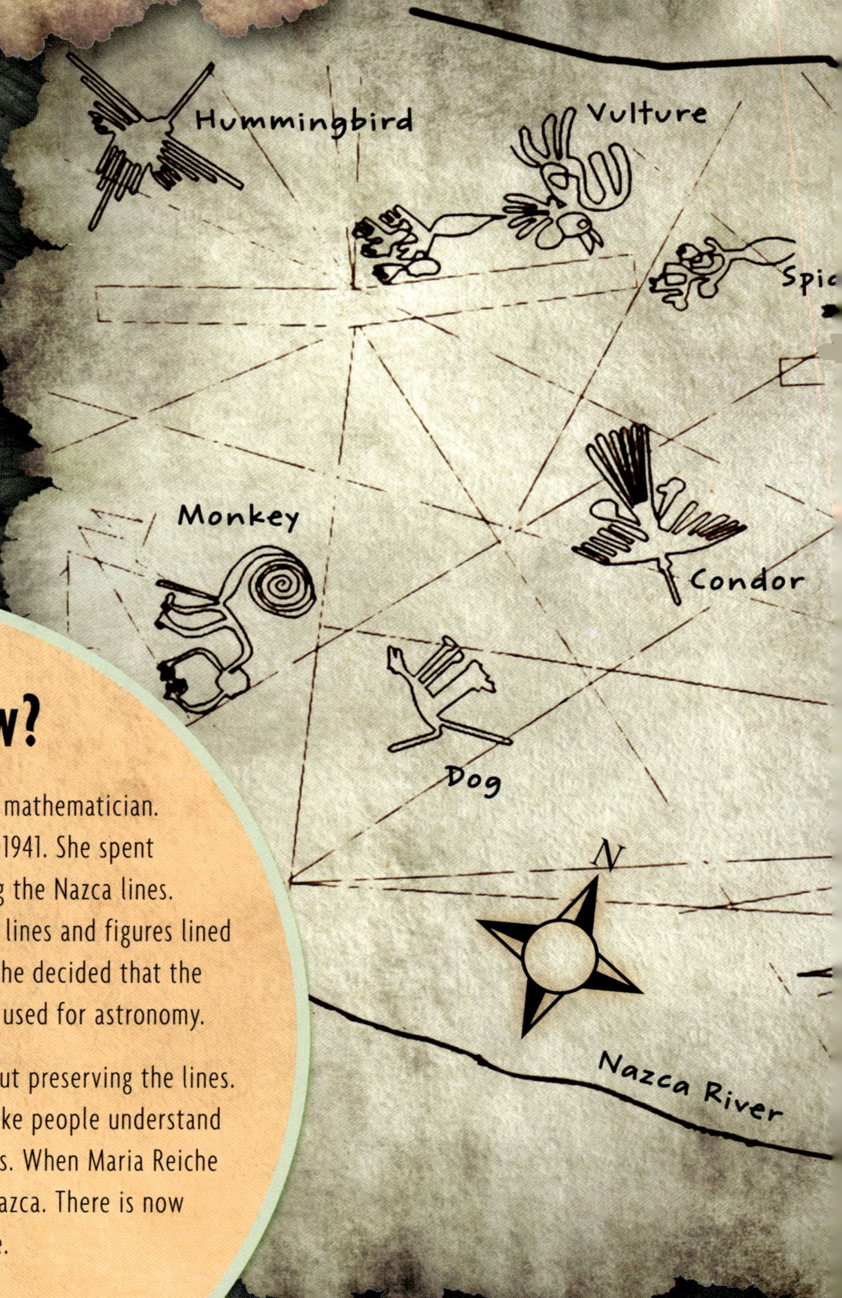

Did You Know?

Maria Reiche was a German mathematician. She went to Nazca, Peru, in 1941. She spent more than 50 years studying the Nazca lines. She found that many of the lines and figures lined up with the sun and stars. She decided that the Nazca lines must have been used for astronomy.

Maria was very worried about preserving the lines. She worked very hard to make people understand the importance of doing this. When Maria Reiche died, she was buried near Nazca. There is now a museum there in her name.

Map of the Nazca Lines and Figures

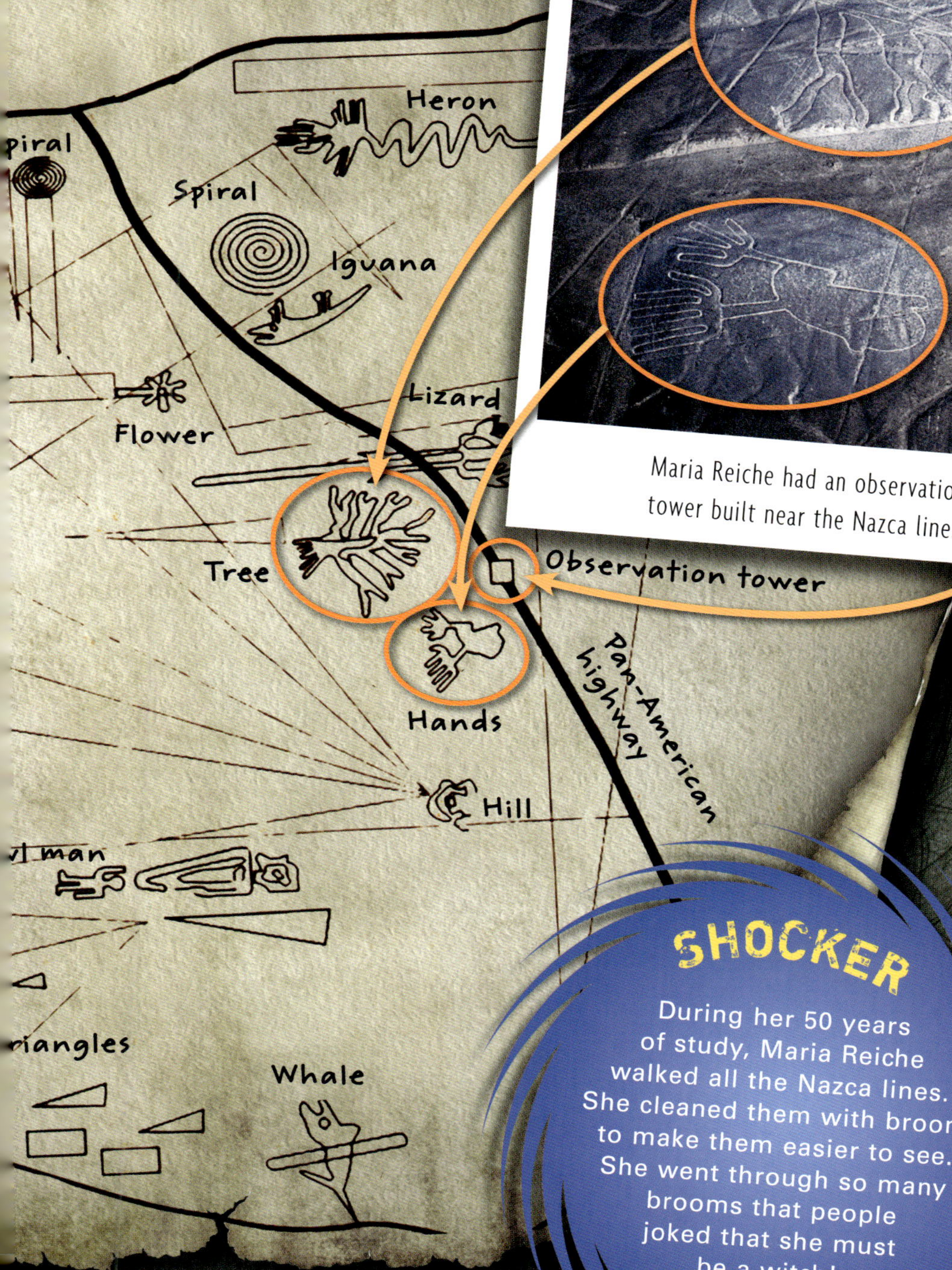

Maria Reiche had an observation tower built near the Nazca lines.

SHOCKER

During her 50 years of study, Maria Reiche walked all the Nazca lines. She cleaned them with brooms to make them easier to see. She went through so many brooms that people joked that she must be a witch!

Places such as Chichén Itzá, Brown Mountain and Stonehenge have always fascinated and puzzled people. Modern science has helped to solve some of these puzzles. As science advances, we understand more and more about the world's mysterious places.

WHAT DO YOU THINK?

Do you think that we will be able to explain all of the world's mysterious places with science?

PRO

Most things today can be explained with science. Our understanding of the world keeps improving thanks to science. It is only a matter of time until we can explain everything with facts and technology.

Stonehenge

However, **logic** and science haven't been able to explain everything. For example, scientists and historians have been studying Stonehenge for hundreds of years. To this day, no one knows for sure why it was built. Most people believe that we may never unlock all the mysteries of the world.

CON

Science can suggest possible explanations for the world's mysterious places. However, we can't say for sure what ancient people thought or felt. Because we can't travel back in time, we can only use our imaginations.

Go to **http://library.thinkquest.org/CR0211481/** to learn more about mysterious places.

GLOSSARY

ancestor a family member who died long ago

archaeologist a scientist who studies the objects of the past

basalt a dark, fine-grained volcanic rock

butte a mountain with steep sides and a flat top that stands by itself

cultural having to do with the beliefs and customs of a group of people

doom a terrible or unhappy fate

equinox one of the two days of the year when day and night are equally long all over the world, due to the position of the sun

extinct no longer erupting, if used in reference to a volcano

geologist a scientist who studies the rocks, minerals and soil of the earth

Gulf Stream a warm, swift current in the Atlantic Ocean

lintel a stone laid flat across the top of two or more standing stones

meteorologist a scientist who studies the atmosphere, focusing on weather and forecasting

monolith a large block of stone

navigation finding the way when travelling, often with the help of maps, compasses or the stars

pyramid a massive monument with a square base and four triangular walls, with inner burial chambers

quarry a place where stone or minerals are dug from the ground

sacrifice an offering to a god or gods of something precious

shroud to cover or hide

solstice the two days of the year, one in June and one in December, when the day is shortest or longest, due to the position of the sun

INDEX